# WHERE THE HECK'S SALTBURN?

*Memories of childhood holidays*
*in a North Yorkshire seaside town*

M A R T I N   J O N E S

Published in the United Kingdom 2016
by Martin Jones

Copyright © 2016
Martin Jones

ISBN  978-0-9935522-0-5

**Special Note from the Author:**
*All profits from the sales of this book will be donated to
Teesside Hospice to help them continue their vital work
in the local community.*

# Contents

# Acknowledgements

Much of the material for this book has come from my own memory and family sources. Nevertheless, I would like to offer grateful thanks to friends and colleagues from my local U3A, in particular Gordon Roxby and Neil Smith, for their help and advice in preparing the book for publication. Also, this book would not have been published without the help, patience and cajoling of my wife Marta, and I am truly grateful to her.

MARTIN JONES


*Printed by Delmar Print*

# Introduction

"Saltburn? Where the heck is Saltburn?" I am sure my 1960's grammar school friends in leafy Surrey could have been forgiven for asking this question when I told them that we were going there again for our summer holidays. After all, for a 'southern softie' family to venture to the north east of England for their holidays would have been regarded as decidedly odd in those days. So why, for many years, did we forgo the undoubted delights of the south coast for the windswept sands of a small North Yorkshire town called Saltburn-by-the Sea? And why would I want to write a book about my experiences of a town which I have visited countless times over the years but have never actually lived in? I invite you to read on.

# A FINE BEACH AND
# WHERE IT ALL BEGAN

My family's connection with Saltburn arose through my father, Trevor and his parents, Everett and Maud Jones. My grandparents were married in July 1915 and lived throughout their married lives of 54 years in a semi-detached house in Raby Road, Stockton-on-Tees. Dad came into the world in October 1916, and it soon became clear that he was very bright, so much so that there were high hopes in the family that he would go to university when he left the local Secondary (Higher Grade) School in 1933. However the recession which swept the area at the start of the 1930's meant that grandpa Jones lost his job with the local Craig Taylor's shipyard, and dad had to go south to try and seek his fortune, and support the family back home with a London-based job in the Civil Service. He was never to return to the area on a permanent basis.

Shortly after he retired from the Civil Service in 1978, dad wrote a book entitled, 'The Story of My Family', a detailed history of the Jones family prepared in days long before genealogy and family histories became a popular online activity. In it, he set down some personal reminiscences from his North Eastern childhood and youth, including seeing the total eclipse of the sun at Marske in June 1927 and walking along the 'fine beach' to Saltburn two miles further down the coast. Holidays at Saltburn began in 1931 or 1932 when dad stayed with the Cotton family, although I do not know whereabouts in Saltburn this would have been. These holidays must have continued after dad went south to find work because he reported that during the last of the holidays in August 1939, he received a telegram ordering him to report back to London immediately. The outbreak of the Second World War followed less than a month later.

In 1940, after his return from France, dad became engaged to my mother Nancy, a South Londoner whom he met at work. By then, holidays at Saltburn were out of the question but photos show that dad and mum visited Saltburn in 1941, presumably as part of a visit to see his parents in Stockton. Shortly after, dad was posted to the Middle East and it was to be another four years before my parents were able to marry and settle down in the family home in South London, a home which (like my grandparents) they were to own throughout their married lives of 45 years.

My older sister Margaret came on the scene in August 1946 and I followed three years later in December 1949. I am not sure how much Saltburn featured in those early post-war years, I am sure it did, but I do know that I was introduced to the town in the summer of 1952 at the tender age of two. My lifelong love affair with Saltburn had begun!

Fairy Glen and train on Riftswood Viaduct, July 1941

# SANDCASTLES, IODINE AND 'PRINCE CHARLES'

## - SALTBURN IN THE 1950'S

For reasons which will become evident later, I have divided my childhood memories of Saltburn into two distinct parts - the 1950's and the 1960's.

In the 1950's, like many families, we were car-less, and journeys to places such as Saltburn had to be undertaken by train or other public transport. Getting from South London to North Yorkshire by train was no mean feat in those days for a family of four, later to become five with the arrival of my younger brother Philip. First of all, we had to persuade the always grumpy booking clerk at our local station to issue the tickets and reserve our seats for the journey, a task in itself, and of course cash had to be handed over for the fares, no computer generated tickets or credit cards in those days! My dad's wartime trunk would be filled to the brim with all we needed for 2-3 weeks and this would be sent off a few days in advance on a British Railways lorry, hoping no doubt that it would arrive in Saltburn before we did. The police were always notified of our absence, water turned off and then we were off to our local station in a taxi at the start of another great annual adventure!

I have always had a soft spot for Kings Cross station in London, this being to my mind the real start point for our holidays in the North East. In the 1950's, the station was always filled with smoke and noise as the steam engines waited their turns and I recall dad pointing out the famous A4 Pacific, Mallard, holder of the world speed record for a steam locomotive. Having found our reserved seats on the train, we awaited our departure into the cavernous smoke-filled depths of the tunnel at the end of the platform.

As a train enthusiast from an early age, I have many memories of our trips north. As the journey normally covered the middle of the day, we would have lunch in the restaurant car - green pea or Brown Windsor soup followed by roast lamb with all the trimmings. Stops might be made at Peterborough and Grantham, the train would slow for the Selby curve and a stop made at York. And then, after what seemed like an age to an excited and impatient youngster, we arrived at Darlington and prepared to change trains.

In the 1950's, the Saltburn trains from Darlington were invariably steam hauled, with a rake of elderly red single-compartment coaches conveying passengers to their destinations along the line. For me, the highlight of the one hour journey was going past the smoke and flames of the furnaces and chimneys at the Teesside steelworks. Stops were made at stations such as Dinsdale, Thornaby, Middlesbrough, Cargo Fleet, Grangetown, and Redcar Central, with its overall roof on the Saltburn platform; and then, as the excitement mounted, the final stop was made at Marske and the church and cliffs at Saltburn came into view. We were nearly there!

On my recent visits to the town, I have always been struck how much Saltburn station has changed over the years. Now there is just a single island platform and two tracks, with a small shelter for intending passengers to use and no station staff on duty. In the 1950's, however, there were four platforms plus a separate 'excursion' platform, where the car park is now situated, which was used by special trains that conveyed day trippers to and from places such as Blackpool. On a steam-hauled train, we always hoped to arrive at platform 1, with its overall roof and fully staffed ticket office, as this enabled us to see the engine draw forward to a former station exit and buffers adjacent to the Zetland Hotel before reversing to the other end of the train. Sidings were abundant at the station, there was a signal box which controlled a number of semaphore signals at the end of the platforms, with another less than a mile away at Tofts Farm, and there was even a small engine shed to service the engines. How times have changed!

The final part of our journey was made, not by train, bus or taxi, but on foot, our destination being nearby Ruby Street. To do this, we went via the old subway under the railway line, left along Milton Street, past the butcher's shop and into Ruby Street. Now we really were there!

Our final destination was 38 Ruby Street, an unassuming and fairly typical terrace house halfway down the street on the left. There we were greeted by our hosts, Mr and Mrs Burton. The Burtons, as I remember them, were a quiet, fairly elderly and friendly couple. Mr Burton was quite disabled and had a job as gatekeeper on the old Halfpenny Bridge, useful to know when we wanted a free passage across the toll bridge! Mrs Burton looked after the house and guests and provided three cooked meals a day, at 9am, 1pm and 6pm. The couple lived in the house, and there was only one bedroom at the front available to guests, hence a squeeze for a young and growing family plus luggage and pushchairs. There was a lounge downstairs which we used, but definitely no TV, DVD or Wi-Fi, so we had to amuse ourselves in the evenings with board games and the like if we were not going out.

Ruby Street in the 1950's was much the same as it is now, the big difference being the absence of cars in those days which enabled us to kick a football or tennis ball around in the street without incurring personal danger or the wrath of motorists. I have already mentioned the butcher's shop at the top of the street, then as today in the hands of the Gosnay family, and there was a second shop and the Ruby Street fish and chip café further down the street on our side, whilst at the top of the street on the opposite side was the Ruby Street Social Club. There were several guest houses in the street catering for the many holidaymakers who came to the town during the main summer holidays. The more modern flats and houses at the bottom of the street were not of course there in the 1950's, and I recall that the area now occupied by the flats was undeveloped and a bit of a wasteland. The cobbled stone alleyways linking the street with other streets were well used by youngsters such as myself at play, and I recall the house walls bordering the alleyways getting quite a battering from footballs and tennis balls!

Saltburn itself has changed little over the years, which is perhaps not surprising given that it has tried to model itself on a Victorian town. Most of the hotels and guest houses, including the large and prominent Alexandra and Zetland Hotels, are now flats, and there have been quite extensive developments close to the pier in connection with the growth of water-based activities in the town. However the upper and lower promenades and connecting paths and steps have changed little from how I remember them in the 1950's; the cliff tram continues to convey trippers to and from the lower promenade; the pier is still in operation, if somewhat truncated in length; and the miniature railway continues to take passengers out to the Italian Gardens, even if the old Halfpenny Bridge and metal tunnel are no longer there as they were in former days. More about these shortly.

So how did we occupy our time over 2-3 weeks in Saltburn in the 1950's, given that we had no car to get us around and there was no TV to stay in and watch when the weather was inclement? I suppose I might be scratching my head for ideas at this point, but I'm not, because we always seemed to have things to do, even when the cold wind swept along the sands from Teesside and the rain and sea mist made playing on the beach a less-than-attractive proposition.

The beach was of course the focus of our activities, and scarcely a day went by when we did not visit the beach at all. Having consumed Mrs Burton's full English breakfast, including bacon and black pudding, we joined the throng of holidaymakers heading down the steps to the lower promenade. At the bottom of the steps, there was a building where green upright tents with wooden bases could be hired, which were always useful for changing and shelter, along with deckchairs, and these were put up close to the Hazelgrove slipway. Windbreaks were also available but I cannot recall using them much. The area at the bottom of the steps also had chalets to hire, which I do not think we ever did in the 1950's, a tea kiosk which dispensed welcome hot drinks in real cups plus white bread sandwiches with cheese slices (delicious!), and some decrepit and smelly toilets which were best avoided particularly when the water supply failed or reduced which it often seemed to do in those days!

A few years ago, I saw a film of some early-1960's celebrations at Saltburn, more on that shortly, and there were the green tents on the beach and buildings and chalets on the lower promenade, now all sadly a distant memory.

The building of sandcastles and digging of trenches and holes 'to Australia' was a daily activity on the beach, and depending on the tides, it was always fun to see the trenches and holes fill up with water and the castles disappear as the sea came in. The inevitable pushchair was pressed into service drawing out 'train lines' in the sand, including points and sidings (I was not the only train enthusiast in the family!), and plastic footballs and tennis balls were often used although the footballs could sometimes be seen heading in the direction of the pier and Huntcliff when the wind was strong and blowing down the beach from Teesside.

I have always had a regard for people who, come rain or shine, swim or surf in the North Sea. I cannot remember the last time that I even dipped my toes in the water, but swimming in the sea was another almost daily ritual for us in the 1950's. I cannot say it was warm, it definitely wasn't, and of course there were no whole-body surfing suits available to us in those days, but I recall we were always keen, as children often are, to have a dip and we were disappointed when the red flag prevented us from going in.

At times of low tide, we often headed to the rock pools under Huntcliff to search for crabs and shrimps, a timeless activity for young and old, and this was inevitably followed by a ride on the nearby swing-boats, a session watching a Punch & Judy show or riding the donkeys on the beach close to the pier, or a visit to the ice cream kiosk and pier when the incoming tide made further crab hunting and beach activities impossible.

On the other side of the beck to the rock pools and swing-boats was the love of my life, the Saltburn Miniature Railway, and a daily ride on the railway, headed by the model A4 Pacific, Prince Charles (or 'tiddly engine' as we knew it), was regarded as a 'must' in the 1950's. In those days, the line started on the promenade side of the beck, and there was a small kiosk, close to where a café is situated now, where a lady dispensed paper tickets to ride the line. The station, called Cat Nab, had a low stone platform and canopy roof, and wooden semaphore signals stood at the end of the platform, although needless to say, they did not operate. There was a run-round facility for the engine at Cat Nab (and at the other end of the line) and the coaches were open-top with wooden bench seats facing both ways. The driver was usually a fairly portly gentleman with glasses and a brown overall-type jacket, and he could sometimes be persuaded to allow young children to sit in the engine seat whilst the train was waiting to fill up with passengers. The first part of the short journey took us past the old engine and carriage shed and into a short metal tunnel in which of course we would always scream! The massive metal Halfpenny Bridge passed over the top of the train and the beck was crossed on a low bridge before the train curved round a bend, with some lovely aromas from the lineside vegetation, and into the station close to the Italian Gardens. These Gardens were (and still are) always kept in pristine condition and were well worth a visit, and the wooden café was often visited before we headed back. And if we had time, we sometimes walked through the Valley Gardens woods, where I know mum and dad walked in 1941, towards the massive brick-built railway viaduct at Riftswood.

I have always had a soft spot for the miniature railway and the Gardens, and I was disappointed when I heard of the railway's later demise due to financial cutbacks. How pleased I was that the closure was only temporary and the railway reopened – and remains open today - largely due to voluntary effort. My first photo with Prince Charles was in 1953, and I really appreciated being able to take more pictures of the same 'tiddly engine' over sixty years later.

As the purpose of our visits to the North East was to see family and relatives, we were often joined at Saltburn by grandparents and assorted uncles and aunts, great uncles and great aunts. Grandpa Jones often arrived on the beach from the station in a dark suit, shirt and tie, and with a coat and hat on if the weather was chilly. Like dad, he was an active man and could normally be relied on to participate fully in the beach activities, even if he did seem a little over-dressed at times for such activities. Grandma Jones on the other hand always preferred to sit in a deckchair and watch the world going by. Woe betide any young child who had the sniffles or a graze, I think she carried the vapour rub and iodine round with her. A bit of a hypochondriac was our grandma Jones but we loved her nonetheless!

On the beach in the 1950's with Mum and Grandpa Jones

A dip with Dad in the cold North Sea and on the swing-boats

The Saltburn Miniature Railway in the early 1950's

The morning's activities on the beach always came to an end at around 12.30pm as the holidaymakers packed up, laced up their tents and headed back up the steps to the upper promenade and the various guest houses, including our own, which served lunch at 1pm sharp. I am sure this would have been another cooked meal, and I certainly remember a full roast lunch, with all the trimmings including Yorkshire pudding (of course!), being served on a Sunday. As a family with young children, I imagine we must have had a rest after an active morning and full breakfast and lunch, but then it was back to the beach until 5.30pm or on one of the many trips which we undertook whilst we were at Saltburn in the 1950's.

Our 1950's trips out always included visits to my grandparents at Stockton, either on a full day or half day basis. Being car-less, this involved catching the steam train to Thornaby and then taking a No. 4 or 5 Stockton Corporation bus out to a stop close to their home in Raby Road. Dad always tried to avoid going to Stockton on market days, as the buses inevitably filled up with shoppers, and on more than one occasion, I recall two or three full buses passing us by before one stopped, which annoyed dad intensely with two or three young children standing on the pavement beside him! I have many memories of the house and area around Raby Road, the apple tree in the back garden which we used to climb to see the steam engines going past on the nearby freight line, the whistling kettle on the stove, and yet more ball games in the road outside (fortunately the road was a cul-de-sac!) and cobbled-stone alleyways. Dad sometimes took us across the fields to the freight line crossing, where we placed old pennies on the line and waited to see the heavy steam engines squashing them flat. Probably against the health and safety regulations even then, but fun!

Another trip out was to Osmotherley on the edge of the North Yorkshire Moors. This involved yet another steam train ride, this time from Middlesbrough to the old Yarm station, and then a single-decker bus, complete with conductor, out to the moorland village. My abiding memory of one trip was seeing a sheep with horns and being decidedly wary of it, presumably not already having come across many sheep with horns in my short life in the southern suburbs of London!

Sometimes we took the red United bus to Marske and Redcar, had a look round Redcar and then caught the bus or train back to Saltburn. I certainly think we also walked from Saltburn to Marske on occasions, just as my father did in the 1920's, and might even have walked all the way to Redcar, no mean feat for a young family along an often windswept and soft sandy beach.

Then there was the annual trip to Whitby and Robin Hoods Bay, always a highlight of our visits to the North East. As with the trips north, this must have involved quite a bit of planning for dad beforehand. An early breakfast was consumed before we headed to The Square to catch the red single-decker Saltburn Motor Service bus to Brotton. At the station there, tickets were purchased and the arrival of the service to Whitby Town was awaited with anticipation. This inevitably comprised two or three elderly single compartment coaches drawn by a tank engine. The journey to Whitby took us past the coastguard cottages, around Huntcliff (always very close to the cliff edge it seemed), and on through the steel works at Skinningrove to Loftus. Further fine views of the North Sea were enjoyed as the train hugged the coast and cliffs near Staithes, Kettleness and Sandsend, and then the train arrived at Whitby West Cliff, with its water towers and steam train waiting in the other platform to take passengers on to Robin Hoods Bay and Scarborough. At this time however, we always stayed on our train as it headed down the steep incline into Whitby Town station.

After a morning and sandwich lunch in Whitby, we headed back to the station and an early afternoon train to Robin Hoods Bay. At the Bay station, I recall being allowed to stand in the small signal box (still there but long used for other purposes) and return a semaphore signal to danger after the train had departed, something again I am sure would not be allowed on the railways now! The afternoon was spent on the beach and amongst the rock pools of this small coastal village, in those days seemingly quiet even in the height of summer, and then it was back to the station and the 5.25pm return journey direct to Brotton. It would have been 8pm before we finally arrived back in Saltburn on the bus and I think we must have got chips from the Ruby Street café to ward off any overnight pangs of hunger, supper time at No. 38 having long passed!

Of course, all these trips and days out were made with my parents and family. However I also recall being allowed to make short local expeditions on my own from an early age, something which I do not think would happen so much nowadays. I recall scaling the steep stony slopes of Windy Hill and Cat Nab (encouraged rather than discouraged as it is now), standing for what seemed like hours by the station fence watching the steam trains come and go, and walking across the Halfpenny Bridge to see old Mr Burton for a chat when he was on duty in the gatehouse on the far side of the bridge. The halfpenny toll for the journey on foot was never needed! The woods around Hazelgrove were always a good source of play, although on one occasion, I fell and grazed my knee quite badly on the cinder path. I had visions of grandma's iodine appearing, but dad had a much better solution and any germs in the knee were quickly exterminated as I was instructed to take a dip in the cold salt-laden waters of the North Sea! At that time, and until a lot later, the beck running down the slope in Hazelgrove was open to the elements, and there were a lot more trees and vegetation beside the open beck. When the summer weather was hot, the aroma from the beck could be decidedly unpleasant, and I often wonder now what used to go into it! At the bottom of the slope, the beck went underground, and from there to the slipway, there was a tarmac avenue, as there is now, but with long wooden seats and overhead canopies and carefully cut grass and tended flowers on the banks. How times have changed!

Talking of aromas, I must mention the 'Saltburn aroma' which was a general feature of our holidays there in the 1950's and 1960's. To this day, I do not know what the aroma was, but I do know it was distinctive to Saltburn. It would always hit us as we got off the train and left the station at the start of our holidays, and it was always present, whatever the weather. It was not an unpleasant aroma, as in poor drainage, nor was it connected to the steam engines in the station or coal fires which burnt in homes even in the height of summer. It might have come from the many works buildings on Teesside but it seemed to be present whatever the wind direction. It might have come from the sea or perhaps it was a disinfectant used by the Council. I simply do not know, and since the aroma has long disappeared from the Saltburn scene, I will probably never know what it was!

I cannot say the sun always shone on us at 1950's Saltburn, as it is supposed to on childhood holidays, but we enjoyed our time there and were always sad when the time came to repack the trunk, say our farewells to the Burtons for another year and walk back to the station for the long trip home.

All this happened a long time ago and, like many childhood holidays, I am sure we hoped they would go on for ever. However for us, our holidays at Saltburn in the 1950's came to an end in 1957 when dad told us that he was being posted to RAF Changi (now the international airport) in Singapore for three years and we would be accompanying him. Our holiday at Saltburn that year was brought forward to June, no problems with term time holidays in those days, and all the visits to the beach and miniature railway, trips and days out were made as before. Then it was time to say farewell to grandparents, hoping no doubt that they would be around when we got back, and to the Burtons, and a final walk to the station and the journey home. For us as a family, our time at Saltburn in the 1950's was at an end.

# HARD BEDS AND WEEKLY BATHS

## – SALTBURN IN THE 1960'S

Our arrival back in the UK in 1960 coincided with the end of the summer holidays, and with the need to get schools sorted out quickly, there was no possibility of a trip north that year. Thus it was early 1961 before thoughts turned to the North East and a return to Saltburn and Stockton. By then, a number of changes had taken place. Both our grandparents were thankfully still around and active in Stockton, but the Burtons were no longer in Ruby Street, and we heard later that Mr Burton had died in a road accident in the town whilst we were away. We missed them both. Our family was now six in number, with another younger brother Colin waiting to make his first trip north, and we were the proud owners of a large 6-cylinder Ford Zephyr, which had been purchased in Singapore and shipped back with us.

The ownership of a car was a blessing for the family, but it also presented to me a potential problem, since it was assumed that we would all make the journey north by car. Big problem to me as a young and enterprising train enthusiast! The solution proposed by my parents was both simple and brave, I would go on the train on the Friday afternoon 'Tees-Thames Express' direct to Thornaby with my sister, stay overnight with our grandparents at Stockton, and then go to Saltburn on the local train with grandpa on the Saturday afternoon to await the arrival of our parents and brothers in the car. Such a solution, involving an 11-year old boy and his 14-year old sister travelling north from London on their own, might seem foolhardy and frankly crazy now, but it didn't then, and it worked, not only that year but in all the subsequent years that we went to Saltburn as a family. Dad accompanied us to Kings Cross, I then took the lead on the journey north, including taking my sister to the restaurant car for afternoon tea with scones, jam in little pots and three sugar cubes in my tea, and grandpa met us at Thornaby and took us on the bus to Raby Road for the night. It seems clear that I was already a practical young man when it came to trains, and full marks to my parents for saving me from a 13-hour journey of misery round London's crowded South and North Circular Roads and through towns and cities such as Doncaster, Selby, York and Thirsk, with scarcely a dual-carriageway let alone a motorway in sight.

On the Saturday afternoon, a further change became evident as a diesel multiple unit train pulled into Thornaby station to take us out to Saltburn. A few steam engines could still be seen on the journey and a few passenger trains to and from Saltburn were still hauled by steam locomotives, but the majority of trains were now diesel hauled. One advantage to be had from the new trains was that we could sit behind the driver and watch as the train journeyed along the line, through the steelworks and little-used Warrenby Halt and on towards Saltburn.

It must have been a time of excitement and anticipation when we finally arrived back at Saltburn after an absence of four years. However it would also have been a time of some sadness as we made our way, not left out of the subway to Ruby Street and the Burtons, but right to our digs for the next three weeks with Mrs Butler.

To this day, I cannot recall exactly where Mrs Butler lived. I know that it was in one of the 'precious stone' or 'jewel' streets leading down to the promenade, perhaps Amber Street, and that it was a large, old-fashioned three-storey terraced house on the left. However that is as much as I can remember. I cannot recall either whether my parents arrived in the car before or after my sister and I on that Saturday, but I do know that they had a slow and difficult journey and I was glad that I had been allowed to go north by train.

Mrs Butler was a small elderly lady with white hair who lived on her own in the house, friendly but quiet and very deaf. I am not sure how we came to stay with her, but my abiding memories were of a very old-fashioned interior, hard beds, weekly baths (more on that shortly) and a radio which blared out loudly from her quarters. A fairly typical 1960's seaside guesthouse, you might say!

Many of the activities we engaged in during the 1950's were resumed in that first year back at Saltburn, including of course the beach activities and visits to the miniature railway. Grandparents and assorted uncles and aunts continued to visit us on the beach, and Windy Hill continued to be scaled from where there were good views of the station and the railway line heading out towards Riftswood and Skelton.

It was in 1961 that we first met up with some people with whom we became good friends. The Burlinson family came on holiday from Darlington, the Clark family from the East Midlands, and Mr Hutchinson came from Nottinghamshire and often went on the train to visit his family in County Durham. It quickly became clear that we all enjoyed a game of cricket, and for two or three years, regular and often raucous cricket matches were played on the beach close to the Hazelgrove slipway. Everyone on the beach was welcome to join in and even grandpa Jones was sometimes seen to turn his arm over in his jacket and tie! We were always sorry when the incoming tide prevented any further play.

Another friend who came on the scene in those early days back at Saltburn was Ivan. At the time, relations with the 'Iron Curtain' countries were decidedly frosty, but lest it be thought that Ivan was an Eastern European spy living in Saltburn, let me confirm that he was in fact a large slobbery boxer dog. Ivan was a well-known local character. He lived with the Robinsons in Ruby Street (more about them later) and he was regularly seen on his own on the beach visiting holidaymakers and anyone else who would give him affection (and biscuits!). To do this, he had to cross the road on the upper promenade, not so much of a problem as it is now, and make his way down the steps to the lower promenade and beach where his adoring public awaited him. If the day was warm and tiring, Ivan could be seen relaxing at The Ship Inn and supping a bowl of something alcoholic with the locals; and if he was too tired afterwards to climb the steps back up to Ruby Street and home, then he could always sit by the lower station of the cliff tram and wait to board the next tram back up to the upper promenade. I never knew whether any payment was made by the Robinsons for these journeys but I doubt it! That was Ivan and his early departure to 'doggy heaven' was felt with sadness by many locals and holidaymakers.

I am not sure whether we ever partook of boating and canoeing on the beck close to the miniature railway in the 1950's, but we certainly did in the early 1960's, and I recall my brother Philip being accidentally hit in the face with an oar and ending up in the beck with a chipped tooth. Boating activities over for the day I imagine! When the weather was inclement, we gravitated to the amusement arcade at the entrance to the pier, and many a happy hour was spent losing pennies on the slot machines. And finally, the film I have already mentioned was of the centenary celebrations of the railway coming to Saltburn, and showed a 'Miss Saltburn' contest taking place on the lower promenade close to the pier on August Bank Holiday 1961. I am sure we would have been at Saltburn at the time and maybe even on the beach or in the pier arcade, but I am equally sure we would not have been allowed by our parents to view such a spectacle. Whatever next!

Some things about our time at Saltburn never changed but others did, and our horizons were quickly broadened in the early 1960's courtesy of our Ford Zephyr. The 6-cylinder 'Dagenham Tank', with its three gears, bench seats and ability to get up Saltburn bank fully loaded in second gear, quickly made its debut in Raby Road, Stockton, although I recall that I was soon allowed to revert to my favourite train and bus to get to my grandparents on my own. Trips out were made to places such as 'Smells Avenue' in Billingham, so called because of the chemical aromas which pervaded the area, and the isolated fishing piers beyond Redcar and Warrenby Halt, and we always looked forward to an evening viewing the flames and furnaces of the steelworks at close quarters.

Strange, but perhaps the biggest benefit of having a car was that it enabled us to go to the swimming baths at Eston. Learning to swim was regarded as obligatory in Singapore, and since the waters of the North Sea were a great deal colder than their tropical equivalents, we soon sought out alternative swimming facilities close to Saltburn. Eston provided those facilities and from early on, we regularly spent mornings or afternoons there. To get there in the 1960's, I recall we had to go through Marske and Lazenby villages, past the gates of ICI Wilton and then down into the outskirts of Middlesbrough. No dual carriageways or by-passes in those days. As we approached the baths, we would always guess whether a trolley bus was waiting at a terminus stop, although I have no idea where that would have been. An added bonus of attending the baths was that it enabled us to have showers. One thing we found out early on was that old Mrs Butler was loathe to turn on the hot water in the house for more than one evening a week, and with a young and active family around, alternative facilities had to be quickly found. Thankfully the swimming baths proved to be a more-than-satisfactory alternative to a wash and brush-up in the North Sea, particularly as the weather at the time of our holiday at Saltburn in 1961 was uniformly dismal!

Whilst we were in the Middlesbrough area, we sometimes visited the famous Transporter Bridge and had a ride across the Tees on it, accompanied by our car. On one occasion – it must have been later in the 1960's – we were told that you could ask for the security gate to be opened and then climb the steps to the top of the Bridge and walk across the top to the other side. Of course we had to do this, and although the climb up to the top and down again on the other side was scary to say the least, we certainly enjoyed the fine views of Teesside from the top. A big problem arose when we got back down to ground level on the other side and found that the Bridge mechanism had failed whilst we were on top. Our car was of course parked back on the town side of the Bridge, and we had the unenviable choice of either climbing back up and over the Bridge to our start point, or trying to cadge a lift round the long way into the town. It was not really a choice, and I think we must have been totally exhausted by the time we got back across the top of the Bridge and down to the car. I was reminded of this particular marathon when I climbed the Sydney Harbour Bridge a few years ago and saw the badge for the famous Teesside-based Dorman Long bridge-building firm near the top.

From an early age, dad was a keen supporter of Middlesbrough Football Club, and in his family history, he recorded seeing Camsell and Pease in action in his 1920's childhood, as well as being involved in some frightening events as a 10-year old when barriers collapsed during a game and many children were forced on the pitch, with a number of casualties resulting. Although dad rarely got to see his team play after he moved south, he maintained his support for them, and it was to the old Ayresome Park that dad and I ventured on a few occasions whilst we were at Saltburn to see early season League matches. My abiding memory of these trips was of parking our large car, which must have stood out like a sore thumb, in a fairly nondescript road of terraced houses close to the ground, and being immediately assailed by a gang of young children wanting 2/6d to 'look after' the car. Needless to say, we paid up and thankfully the car still had its wheels on when we returned after the match although the children had long since disappeared!

Another trip out which we always enjoyed was to Roseberry Topping, which we climbed on a number of occasions from the car park at Newton-under-Roseberry. The climb up this landmark was always steep and tough, but the views from the top of Teesside and towards the coast were magnificent, and on occasions, a diesel train could be seen rattling along below on the line into Guisborough. I recall it often seemed bitterly cold at the summit, even in summer, and having admired the names carved many years before on the rocks at the top, we quickly headed back down the slope to the comparative warmth of the car park and car.

In that first year back in Saltburn, I kept looking for signs of passenger trains running round Huntcliff towards Loftus and Whitby as they did in the 1950's, but of these trains, there was no sign; and a run along the coast in the car towards Staithes quickly confirmed that we would not be catching the 9.52am steam train from Brotton to Whitby Town that year or ever again, the line having closed whilst we were abroad. Henceforth, our trips to Whitby and Robin Hoods Bay would need to be made by other means.

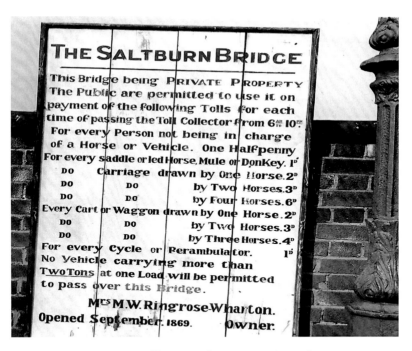

# THE SALTBURN BRIDGE

This Bridge being PRIVATE PROPERTY The Public are permitted to use it on payment of the following Tolls for each time of passing the Toll Collector from 6 AM to 10 PM.

For every Person not being in charge of a Horse or Vehicle. One Halfpenny
For every saddle or led Horse, Mule or Donkey. 1ᴰ
DO     Carriage drawn by One Horse. 2ᴰ
DO     DO     by Two Horses. 3ᴰ
DO     DO     by Four Horses. 6ᴰ
Every Cart or Waggon drawn by One Horse. 2ᴰ
DO     DO     by Two Horses. 3ᴰ
DO     DO     by Three Horses. 4ᴰ
For every Cycle or Perambulator.     1ᴰ
No Vehicle carrying more than Two Tons at one Load will be permitted to pass over this Bridge.

Mrs M.W. Ringrose Wharton.
Opened September. 1869.     Owner.

1960's - Halfpenny Bridge entrance sign and on top of the Transporter Bridge in Middlesbrough

Dad always had a love of the coast and moors, and having a car meant that he could pursue this love in family days out on the moors. This was always planned for a Thursday, but why, might you ask, did it have to be a Thursday? The answer was because Mrs Butler always turned the hot water on in the house on a Thursday and only on a Thursday, and we did not have to rely on a visit to the showers at the swimming baths as a result. Strange but true. I think we made two or three Thursday trips out in 1961, and on each occasion, the weather was foul. We may have been fascinated as 'southern softies' by the snow posts and cattle grids, but being stuck in a car on narrow winding moorland roads on miserably wet misty days was certainly no fun and tempers became quickly frayed. Wisely perhaps, dad reached into his pocket the following year and I was able to take train rides on my own whilst the rest of the family enjoyed shorter trips out in the car.

I cannot recall our 1961 visit to Saltburn as being a great success, it wasn't, and I cannot recall either whether it was through choice or necessity that we decided not to return to Mrs Butler the following year. However that decision was made and it was to Mr and Mrs Blackwell that we headed in 1962.

As with Mrs Butler, I cannot recall exactly where Mr and Mrs Blackwell lived, although I do know that it was (again) in one of the 'jewel' streets leading down to the upper promenade. The couple were middle-aged and, unlike the Burtons and Mrs Butler, they had family (and a dog) there as well. The house was a terrace, and as with the Burtons and Mrs Butler, it comprised a typical 1950's / 1960's guest house, lacking many of the facilities which holidaymakers take for granted nowadays.

For the first time, I am scratching my head now to remember what new activities we might have undertaken in 1962. As a 12-year old, I certainly headed out on the train to Middleton-in-Teesdale and Richmond, both via Darlington, on lines that have long since closed. However the through trains from Saltburn to Blackpool and destinations in the North West and Lakes had ended the previous summer, and it has always been a source of disappointment to me that I did not have the opportunity to take one of these trains across the Pennines via Stainmore on a line which closed in early 1962. Saltburn to Penrith (for Keswick) for 7/6d half return would have been an extremely attractive proposition for me, even with a 4.55am start from Saltburn, but it was not to be!

I believe that it was in 1962 that we first headed to the Cosy Cinema. The lack of facilities, including TV, in Saltburn guest houses at the time was undoubtedly a problem. Going to the cinema was already a popular 1960's activity for many children, and my brothers, sister and I had spent many a Saturday morning attending matinees at our local cinema in South London. Thus, an evening at Saltburn's one and only cinema seemed a good thing to do, given the lack of alternatives and the often dismal weather outside; and this became a regular feature of our holidays at Saltburn, although for the life of me, I cannot remember what films we might have seen there! Close by the cinema was a Social Club, with the smell of beer and cigarette smoke wafting out on to the street on warm evenings, but needless to say, as children we were never allowed to go in! Both these facilities have disappeared from the Saltburn scene, although I am sure they will be remembered by many locals and holidaymakers. I also recall a laundrette close to the cinema and social club which mum used to visit on occasions whilst we were in Saltburn, and which I note is still there today. Such mundane activities as washing clothes might have passed us by as children on holiday, but of course they were essential activities if a family was to look even remotely presentable during 2-3 weeks by the sea!

On one Sunday morning, Tyne Tees Television came to town to broadcast an outdoor church service from the beach close to the Hazelgrove slipway and chalets. The service was broadcast live and of course we had to be there to be part of what turned out to be a sparse and somewhat unenthusiastic 'congregation'. The problem of being on live TV was that we were unable to see ourselves on television, and of course there were no recording or playback facilities available in those days. How I wish the service had been twenty or thirty years later!

Talking of media, I recall waiting with anticipation for the cry 'Evening Gazette!' to go up as the newspaper seller walked round the town selling his wares. His cry could be heard from the beach. The Saturday evening late edition was awaited with particular interest as the 'stop press' usually included the football results and I could see how my beloved Crystal Palace had got on in their opening fixtures of the season. No 24-hour TV sports news in those days of course, and I recall it was a lot later before my team started to be seen on the likes of Match of the Day!

During our stay at Saltburn in 1962, I was walking along the upper promenade when I noticed a boy from my grammar school, Steve, approaching from the other direction. Both of us were there on holiday – in his case staying on his own with grandparents – and neither of us was aware that the other was in town. A 'David Livingstone, I presume' moment you might say! Steve was an able cricketer and was happy to join in with the games of beach cricket over the next week or so. His recent death saddened me and brought back memories of our time at Saltburn in 1962.

A memorable incident to me as a rail enthusiast came at the end of our 1962 holiday. As in 1961, my sister and I made the journey by train, and in 1962, this involved taking the summer Saturday through train from Saltburn back to London Kings Cross. This was steam hauled from Saltburn to Stockton where the train joined coaches from South Shields, Sunderland and Hartlepool for the journey south. A complicated manoeuvre was required to effect the combining of the trains which involved the Saltburn train – passengers and all - being shunted forwards to allow the train from the north to enter the station, and then reversing back into the station to join the rear of the train for the journey south. In 1962 and in subsequent years, grandpa joined the train at Stockton for this manoeuvre, and I often wondered what ticket he asked for at the booking office, I suspect it was no more than a 1d platform ticket! Joy-of-joys in 1962 as the train from the north came in headed by that most famous of steam engines, Flying Scotsman, I was in seventh heaven as we made our way south to York and Doncaster where a change to diesel locomotive was made. This was the last time that I saw Flying Scotsman in British Railways days, the engine being withdrawn from service less than a year later, but as the engine was subsequently preserved and used on the main line, I have been able recall that morning at Stockton station with fond memories.

Beach activities, trips out, visits to grandparents and swimming baths, cramped facilities, no TV, dismal weather......... it might have seemed mundane and uninviting, and to an extent it was. And therein lay a problem. What might have been acceptable to a young family in the 1950's was not proving to be acceptable to a growing family in the early 1960's, particularly as we had got used to much better (and warmer!) facilities and activities in our three years overseas. I am sure it must have been mum who suggested a change after our holiday at Saltburn in 1962. Knowing dad, he would have resisted, and anyway, any thoughts of a holiday were put on hold as the coldest, snowiest winter on record took hold of the country in early 1963. I am sure dad must have won the argument because in early April 1963, mum headed to Saltburn for a few days, and came back to tell us that we would be staying that year with Mr and Mrs Robinson in Ruby Street.

I for one was happy with the move. The Robinsons were a well-known local family and Mrs Robinson – Vera I think although we as children (and subsequently as adults) always knew her as 'Mrs Robinson' - ran a guest house towards the bottom of Ruby Street on the opposite side to No 38. I think it would have been No 35 (now flats I believe), but I cannot recall for sure. The Robinsons were always keen on fishing, a popular activity at Saltburn, and I was pleased to see a picture recently of what looked like Mrs Robinson judging a fishing competition on the lower promenade. I think Ivan, the Robinsons' slobbery boxer dog, was still around then but again I cannot be sure.

Our stay back in Ruby Street proved to be short-lived because in 1964, we headed to the Sea View guest house which Mr and Mrs Robinson's daughter, Margaret Noble, had purchased on the upper promenade, Marine Parade, overlooking the sea. I am not sure why we made this move, but I know we were pleased to be able to maintain the connections with the family, a connection which in my case was to last until the 1980's and 1990's, long after Mrs Robinson's death.

A feature of our 1964 holiday was being allowed to take my bike to Saltburn. My father was never keen on car roof racks, and I think I must have taken the bike on the train with me. If I did, I would have needed to cycle across London from Victoria to Kings Cross, bikes on buses and tube trains not being allowed, and the whole process would have been quite a feat for a 14 year old, given that two or three changes of train were involved on the journey north.

Two days out on the bike are recalled. On the first, I took the train to Richmond and then cycled back to Barnard Castle by way of Reeth and Bowes, a journey of many miles across the Upper Pennines. I looked out for the famous Tan Hill Inn and eventually came across it in the swirling mist, and I followed the old A66 adjacent to the old railway line past Stainmore Summit, now subsumed into the dual carriageway which forms part of the busy A66 cross-Pennine route. I must have been exhausted by the time I arrived back at Saltburn in the evening and I am sure it was a trip which would not be undertaken by many 14-year olds nowadays!

The second trip was much more local, to Whitby via the coast and back by way of the main road across the moors. I recall hearing a steam engine at Whitby station but being unable to see it because I needed a ticket to get on the platform! I also recall leaning over a bridge to look at the Scarborough line heading off towards Robin Hoods Bay, a trip which I had last undertaken in 1957. Sadly, a year later, when I looked again, the rails were beginning to rust over, the line to Scarborough having closed the previous March.

The journey back from Whitby across the busy but isolated inland moorland road proved to be a memorable experience, but for all the wrong reasons, as a sudden and heavy thunderstorm, lightning and pouring rain came crashing down on the moors. I might have been used to big thunderstorms from my Singapore days, but never has a teenage boy pedalled across the moors on a bike so quickly, and never has there been such great relief as when the waterworks and roads to Castleton and Skelton came into view on the Guisborough side of the moors!

One small incident comes to mind from the 1964 holiday. I had gone across on my own to my grandparents' home in Stockton, I cannot think whether it was on the bike or train, and my departure from Raby Road for the return journey was delayed for some reason. My grandparents were always enthusiastic TV viewers, watching BBC Channel 1 and Tyne Tees Television Channel 8 on a black and white 405-line TV in their lounge from early on. However, to the best of my recollection, they never had a telephone in the house in all their married years there, and this caused problems, notably now when I needed to contact my parents to tell them that I would be late back to Saltburn. There was nothing for it but to venture down to the nearest public phone box, then much more plentiful than they are now, and to ring the guest house at Saltburn. This had the wonderful number, Saltburn 13, and had to be accessed via the operator. In those days of course, there was a Button A and a Button B and perhaps inevitably I either pressed the wrong button or pressed the right button at the wrong time, thereby incurring the wrath of the operator. Strange how this little incident comes to mind now over fifty years later and strange how communications by telephone have moved on since then!

Another strange incident arose later in the 1964 holiday when the sun came out for a few days, jerseys were discarded for T-shirts, and the North Sea became a more appealing alternative to swimming at the Eston baths! I think this must have persuaded my parents to give Saltburn and Margaret's guest house on Marine Parade one more try, and the journey north was made once again in July 1965. This holiday proved to be a bit of a disaster as the weather reverted to type - uniformly dismal – our cricketing friends of previous years had deserted the beach for warmer climes, and the daily rides on the Miniature Railway and trips to the swimming baths became an irritation rather than an attraction to a growing family of boys, my older sister having found other places to go on holiday by then. As we packed up at the end of the holiday in 1965, I think we must have realised that our annual family trips to

Saltburn were coming to an end, and this proved to be the case, as mum put her foot down and announced soon after that we would be going to the south coast in West Sussex in 1966. Our family involvement at Saltburn, which in my case had lasted 13 years, was at an end, or was it....?

1965 was indeed a watershed, and a hot sunny two weeks on the south coast shortly after England won the World Cup in 1966 confirmed this. However 1965 was not to be my last trip to Saltburn in the 1960's, as dad reached into his pocket once more following the completion of my 'A' levels in 1968 and paid for me to go north for a week before I started work in the Civil Service. I had been taking driving lessons at the time, but had not yet passed my test, so it was on the train once again, with pedal bike in tow, that I headed north in August 1968. By then, I think Mr and Mrs Robinson must have moved from Ruby Street round the corner to Crake Hall House on Marine Parade, more about that shortly, however I am sure I stayed again with Margaret at her Sea View guest house further up Marine Parade.

The week was perhaps idyllic, being sandwiched between the world of childhood education in the past and the grinding world of adult work to come. All the attractions were still there, and although I probably did not take daily rides on the miniature railway as a strapping 18-year old, I certainly got out and about on foot, bike and train. And the sun shone.....at least when I spent a relaxing Sunday afternoon watching play at the local Saltburn Cricket Club!

During the stay at Saltburn, I paid a couple of visits to my grandparents in Stockton, and although I was not to know it at the time, these proved to be my final visits to see them at their house in Raby Road. By then, my grandparents were well into their 80's, and in April the following year, grandpa Jones died suddenly whilst dad was staying at Raby Road, and grandma Jones followed less than a year later. Both had been an integral part of our family holidays at Saltburn since my earliest days, and their passing left a considerable void in our lives. I missed them both.

A month after I ventured north in 1968, I entered the world of work and a career in the Civil Service lasting over 30 years. For the first time, I was earning my own money rather than relying on pocket money and handouts from my parents, and soon after I passed my driving test, thereby presenting me with greater opportunities to travel. My childhood days were well and truly over. So did this mean the end of my time at Saltburn? I invite you to keep reading for a little longer.

# DEATH AND RE-BIRTH IN SALTBURN,1970 TO 2000

I am minded that the title at the start of this book talks of 'childhood memories' of Saltburn, but I want to continue these memories of a place which has been an big part of my life in childhood and adulthood. I hope you will understand.

Of all the decades in my life, the 1970's was certainly the one in which I was least involved with Saltburn. By then, I was fully immersed in the world of work, and although I was not tempted to use my hard-earned monthly salary to fund travel to exotic overseas locations on the new budget airlines such as Laker, I was able to visit many more parts of Britain, often travelling by a combination of train, bus and foot to get there.

I can only remember two visits to Saltburn during this decade. The first was in the summer of 1970, just a couple of years after I had last visited the area, and I recall that I turned up in my parents' by-now elderly Ford Zephyr car, my Civil Service salary being insufficient to fund a car of my own.

By then, changes were already taking place. Both my grandparents had died since my last visit in 1968 and their family home in Raby Road had been sold for the first time in 54 years, and this particularly saddened me after almost twenty years of visiting them in Stockton and watching out for them as they descended the steps to the beach at Saltburn. The holidaymakers who had flocked to the resort in the 1950's and 1960's were now beginning to use their hard-earned cash on cheap foreign holidays, and the beach seemed strangely deserted, even in the height of summer, with the familiar green tents fast disappearing from the scene.

I cannot recall whether I stayed at the Sea View Guest House or Crake Hall House in 1970, but my abiding memory of that visit was of a night of pouring rain and gale force winds which forced me to switch rooms in the dead of night as the water poured in through the sash windows in my sea-facing room. And this was in the height of summer, no wonder cheap foreign holidays were beginning to prove an attractive alternative to the beach at Saltburn!

By the time of my next visit to Saltburn in 1973, the changes in the town were gathering pace. Hotels and guest houses were beginning to disappear from the scene, and those that remained were required to cater for guests other than holidaymakers in order to survive. The Robinson family had always welcomed Redcar race-goers to their premises and in the 1970's, they also started taking in professional singers and dancers from touring rep companies, including at least one Russian ballet company whilst they were performing on Teesside. Different but interesting I am sure!

I enjoyed my 1973 visit, partly because the sun shone most of the week and I was able to get out on long walks on the coast and moors. I think it must have been May 1973 when I visited because I recall seeing children in uniforms at play in schools which have long since disappeared from the local scene. On the one wet day of that week, I ventured across to Grosmont to have a ride on the newly opened North Yorkshire Moors Railway. It poured with rain all day and the moorland scenery lacked interest as a result, and I don't think I ever appreciated for a minute how much the Railway would become a part of my later life, more on that shortly.

I was not to know it at the time but my 1973 visit was to be the last time I met Mrs Robinson and the last time that I saw a familiar landmark which had been part of my life since my earliest days there. The Halfpenny Bridge was by then showing alarming signs of deterioration, with bits falling into the valley below, and in late 1974, the decision was taken to literally blow it up, which of course attracted a lot of national media attention when it happened shortly before Christmas that year. The decision was inevitable but I was saddened at the loss of this familiar and popular local landmark, and to this day, I recall with fondness my early trips across the bridge and my visits to see old Mr Burton at work in the gatehouse on the far side.

The destruction of the bridge was recorded in a short TV film entitled End of the Pier which was made in 1986 and is (at the time of writing) available to view online in the British Film Institute's film archives. The pier, which was the main feature of the film, was closed for a time in the 1970's and reduced in length and the Miniature Railway ceased operation, and although both have happily been revived and survive to the present, I certainly believe that the 1970's was a time of change at Saltburn and perhaps marked a period of wilderness for the town, a period which was to extend into the 1980's when efforts were at last made to restore the town to something like its former glory.

My parents continued to stay at Crake Hall House during the 1970's, first of all with Mrs Robinson and then with her daughter Margaret who took over there when Mrs Robinson retired from the guest house business. In 1978, my father retired from the Civil Service after a career lasting some 45 years, and at about this time, he and mum began to stay at a guest house at Goathland near Whitby rather than Saltburn. A couple of years later I followed them to Goathland and began an association with that pretty moorland village which has lasted to the present. I cannot think when my parents last stayed at Saltburn, I am sure it must have been in the late 1970's, but when they left for the last time, it certainly seemed that a family era had at last some to an end. Or had it?

It was to be May 1981 before I returned to Saltburn and then it was only for a day trip. By then, I was staying at Goathland, on the other side of the moors and close to my beloved North Yorkshire Moors Railway. One Sunday, I was not feeling 100%, so decided to head to Saltburn for a relaxing afternoon as an alternative to striding the moors. The day was sunny and warm but it was early season, and I was expecting to find the beach and promenade fairly quiet, as they might have been during the 1970's. How wrong I was, with crowds of Sunday day-trippers on the pier, beach and promenade, and the cliff tram doing brisk business ferrying families between the upper and lower promenades. I was surprised, but perhaps I should not have been, the changing economic climate making days out at places like Saltburn a more attractive proposition than in the 1970's, particularly for families. These were not holidaymakers as we would have known them in the 1950's and 1960's, but they were clearly welcome as the resort tried to revive its fortunes. I was pleasantly surprised and decided to visit again.

My next visit in 1983 was my first stay back in the resort for ten years. By then, Margaret at Crake Hall House was only offering bed & breakfast, but this did not prove to be a problem as a few of the local pubs/hotels offered good evening meals, and Margaret provided a full English breakfast, including all the trimmings, which obviated the need for lunch or afternoon tea.

The following January, I returned to Crake Hall House for a few nights on my way to Newcastle on business. This was to be my first and only experience of Saltburn in winter, and although it was dry throughout my stay, it was also perishing cold for a 'southern softie' like me, with coats and hot water bottles unable to assuage my overriding feeling of numbing chill by day and night. I must apologise to the year-round residents of Saltburn, but it was not an experience that I cared to repeat!

Desolation in the Valley as an empty-looking Miniature Railway train heads towards the doomed Halfpenny Bridge, May 1973

A few years later, the Railway had closed

Scenes at a quiet Saltburn in the early 1980's

1986 was a significant year in Saltburn's history, being 125 years since the railway first came to the town. In August of that year, a Victorian Week was held in the town, marking a focus on Saltburn's Victorian heritage; and when it was announced that there would be a steam train trip from Newcastle to Saltburn on the Sunday of the Victorian Week, with a trip out round Huntcliff to Skinningrove thrown in, I decided that I had to be there!

The trip to Saltburn from Newcastle via Stockton behind steam engine number 2005 was less-than-memorable, being beset by delays due to Sunday engineering works, but as we came past Tofts Farm and saw the crowds of people lining the trackside to greet us, it all became worthwhile making the long trip from the south of England via Newcastle to be there.

If it had been the 1950's or 1960's, we would no doubt have gone straight into the old platform 1 or even the excursion platform, but by the 1980's, Saltburn station had been cut back to the present one island platform and two tracks, and we had to wait outside the station for half-an-hour until the service train left for Darlington. Any annoyance on my part as we waited quickly disappeared as my ticket came up as the winner of the train raffle and a footplate ride on the North Yorkshire Moors Railway beckoned. And then we arrived in the 'new' platform 2 of Saltburn station, my first arrival behind a steam engine for some 25 years, and prepared to leave the train amidst the scrum of people already on the platform. I stuck around the station for a while taking pictures of the engine before heading down to the upper promenade to enjoy the early afternoon events.

Then the crowds returned at last – Victorian Sunday 1986

The train arriving at platform 2...steam at Saltburn station

The steam train left Saltburn.....

...and we went on the diesel train past the lonely
coastguard cottages on Huntcliff

The crowds enjoyed themselves on the upper promenade...

... and on the lower promenade and beach

The Sunday of that first Victorian Week was memorable, with local residents dressed in Victorian clothes, strolling up and down the promenades as people might have done a century before, and crowds of day-trippers watching what was going on.

I stayed for a while before heading back to the station and the trip round Huntcliff on the freight line towards Boulby Mine. I cannot recall whether the steam engine was ever due to head the train, probably not, but in the event, a 'Pacer' diesel unit was in the station platform waiting to take the passengers on the trip. Any disappointment on my part quickly disappeared as I prepared to make a journey which I had last made from Brotton in 1957. In days gone by, a few through trains had operated in summer from Saltburn to Whitby via Brotton, and I imagine these must have reversed outside of Saltburn station to take the Skinningrove line towards Skelton and Loftus. However these trains had ceased in the 1950's and the signal boxes controlling the crossovers had long been taken out, and so it was to Redcar that we first headed before we could cross over and come back to Saltburn junction and the freight line to Skelton.

I do not know when the last passenger train ran on this line, it might have been up to thirty years before, and the crowds of local residents and enthusiasts on the train clearly felt like excited pioneers as the diesel train headed out across the Riftswood viaduct and past the site of the former station at Skelton. Brotton station, where we had waited for the 9.52am steam train to Whitby in the 1950's, was passed, with the station building and platforms still intact over twenty five years after the last train had departed. Then it was on to Huntcliff, now single line rather than double as it was in former days, past the former coastguard cottages (now demolished) and hugging the cliff as I remembered it from the 1950's, and on round the clifftop towards Skinningrove. If there was one small disappointment with the trip, it was that the journey ended at the signal box close to the Skinningrove works, the line beyond that to the private potash mine at Boulby being closed for traffic on that Sunday, and it was to be another four years before I finally headed back through Loftus and the Grinkle tunnel to Boulby. However it was a memorable trip for me and I was clearly not alone in welcoming the opportunity to revisit old haunts from long ago.

Back in Saltburn, I re-joined the crowds of people watching the Victorian events before heading back to the station and the trip home at the end of a memorable day. I was not to know it, but I heard later that shortly after I left, the Ruby Street fish and chip café caught fire and closed for good, bringing to an end a personal link with Ruby Street and Saltburn which had lasted for over thirty years.

By 1988, I was beginning to tire of life in the south of England, with its over-crowding and frenetic pace of life, and I first began to have thoughts of moving north. That summer, I stayed for a few days with Margaret at Crake Hall House and made some enquiries. However these came to nothing and it was to be another twelve months before thoughts turned to reality.

I enjoyed my 1988 stay at Crake Hall, notably because the sun shone throughout my stay and T-shirts rather than pullovers were the order of the day. I resisted the urge to take a dip in the North Sea but I recall walking all the way from Saltburn to Runswick Bay along the coast one very warm day and finding that there were no buses to take me back to Saltburn due to a strike. As I stood perplexed and concerned at the bus stop, a car stopped and the fairly elderly driver and passenger offered me a lift back, not just to Saltburn but to the door of Crake Hall. On the journey, they told me of their forthcoming visit to a Billy Graham Convention in the north east. Normally I would have been less-than-happy about discussing religion with strangers, but on this occasion, in view of their kindness, I was more than happy to sit and listen. And yes, I did keep my promise to attend the Billy Graham Convention when he came to speak at the Crystal Palace Sports Centre one evening a few weeks later! On the last night of my 1988 stay, as the sun started to set on the warm sands, I walked along the beach from Saltburn to Redcar, as my father might have done fifty to sixty years before. I was not to know it at the time, but this was to be my last night's stay in Saltburn.

The late 1980's and early 1990's were a time of great change for me. In September 1989, as young people packed to go to university for the first time, I too packed up and prepared to move north, not to university, nor to Saltburn or Teesside or even Newcastle, but to Blackpool on the Lancashire coast where a new job awaited me.

The sense of change was abruptly heightened the following February when dad died suddenly at home in the south of England, and I had to return south to help with the funeral arrangements. Another link with Saltburn had been sadly lost, but indirectly this led to my next visit to Saltburn. Dad had always wanted his ashes scattered close to Danby Beacon on the top of the North Yorkshire moors, and my family decided to do this in conjunction with a visit to Saltburn. What better day to visit the town than the Victorian Sunday in August 1990, and so it was that on this day, we scattered dad's ashes high on the moors and then headed to Saltburn. By then, the Victorian Sunday was proving to be very popular, so-much-so that passes were required to park anywhere in the Saltburn area. Our mum was nothing if not resourceful and a telephone call to Margaret at Crake Hall House quickly secured that vital piece of paper. We enjoyed our visit that day, and I recall seeing the Red Arrows (I think it was that year) and riding out to Skinningrove and on to the Boulby Mine on a special train.

I continued to stay at Goathland in the 1990's and regularly crossed the moors to visit Saltburn and Teesside. In 1992, I was persuaded to visit Stockton to see Durham Cricket Club in action with some friends. I recall I had a difficult time finding the Stockton Cricket Club where the match was being played, (no sat-nav in those days!) but as I finally arrived at the ground, I found to my astonishment that it was almost opposite my dad's old school and close to Raby Road where my grandparents had lived throughout their married lives. Cricket had to take a back seat that day as I took a nostalgic trip back into the 1950's and 1960's, and fortunately my friends understood!

On a subsequent visit to Stockton, I had my mum with me and, ever resourceful and far braver than I would have been, she knocked on the door of my grandparents' old house in Raby Road and asked to be shown round. The rather surprised occupants turned out to be very obliging and we spent a nostalgic half-hour recalling where the whistling kettle used to be located and walking round the garden where I had climbed the apple tree some forty years before. We were always grateful that we found such obliging people at the house.

Back to Saltburn, and I think it was in 1996 when I became aware that Crake Hall House was up for sale and Margaret was preparing to retire from the guest house business in which she and her mother Mrs Robinson had been closely involved for so many years. By the time of my next visit, the House had been sold to the Care Home which had been in operation for many years next door, and another link with Saltburn was at an end. I was particularly sad.

In the early 1990's, mum moved to the south coast where she enjoyed eight happy and active years, including two or three visits to see me in Blackpool. When she visited, we always made a point of heading across the Pennines to Goathland and Saltburn, and it was on one of these visits that we met up with Margaret at Crake Hall House for the last time. By the time of her next visit in July 1999, mum was beginning to slow down, but she still insisted on coming by coach from Worthing to the North West to see me graduate from a university course which I had been undertaking in Lancaster. We agreed that I would take her back home via North Yorkshire, and we spent a very pleasant few days looking round our old haunts including Saltburn. I recall we walked up Ruby Street past No. 38 to the station, along the upper promenade past Crake Hall House and Sea View, down on the cliff tram to the lower promenade for a short sit and stroll, and then back up on the cliff tram to the car and the journey home. Three weeks later, mum died at home a few months short of her 80th birthday and, amidst all the grief, I was so, so pleased that I had been able to give her the opportunity to take one last look round the resort which had been an integral part of her life for so many years. Yet another link with Saltburn, which in mum's case had lasted almost sixty years, had come to an end.

Mum pays a last visit to her beloved Saltburn, July 1999
(pity about the bins!)

and less than a year later, we remembered her on the pier

# A NEW MILLENNIUM
# AND NEW BEGINNINGS

In December 1999, I celebrated my 50th birthday, and a few days later, a new millennium was ushered in amidst much celebration. For my family though, there was one last sad task we needed to carry out for our mum, and in March 2000, we travelled to her beloved North Yorkshire moors to scatter her ashes near to Danby Beacon and then headed to Saltburn as we had done ten years before. Unlike August 1990, it was quiet that weekday afternoon on the lower promenade, and as we sat and reflected awhile at the end of the pier, it felt as though the town was grieving silently with us in our loss. We headed home, still sad at our loss but glad that we had been able to fulfil our mum's final wishes.

Changes in my life continued afoot, and later in 2000, I moved to Crewe in Cheshire to be with Marta, who is now my wife of ten years. I think it must have been 2001 or 2002 when I introduced Marta to Saltburn, shades of my dad some sixty years before, and we have both enjoyed making regular trips to the resort ever since.

In 2002, Marta and I purchased a caravan near Whitby, and at about the same time, I finally retired from the Civil Service after a career lasting over thirty years and began working in a local primary school in Crewe. These two combined meant that we were able to enjoy long summer holidays in the North East, including regular visits across the moors to Saltburn. We both also became volunteers on the North Yorkshire Moors Railway which I had first visited just two weeks after it opened in 1973.

In 2007, the Saltburn Miniature Railway celebrated its 60th birthday, and of course I had to be there for the celebration weekend in August of that year. It was good to see a number of miniature engines around that Sunday afternoon, including steam engines and my beloved Prince Charles, and large crowds of people enjoying the event, and full marks to the volunteers for carrying on when the heavens opened midway through the afternoon and conspired unsuccessfully to spoil the celebrations.

A page for my grandparents' house in Raby Road, Stockton and
the old railway line (now a pathway and cycleway) nearby

Steam on the Miniature Railway as it celebrates its
60th birthday, August 2007

I took a ride

...and later tried to re-enact my early 1950's photo with Prince Charles

Four years later in 2011, the railways featured once more as Saltburn celebrated 150 years since the coming of the railway to the town. A number of special events were organised as part of the celebrations, and I was pleased to be able to participate in one of these events, a special train into Saltburn from York in October of that year. The train was due to be steam hauled, but in the event, a perceived 'fire risk' meant that diesel locomotives had to be used instead. The irony of the October drizzle which accompanied much of the journey was not lost on the passengers! A bonus of this trip was that it included another trip out along the freight line to the Boulby Mine via Huntcliff and Skinningrove, my third trip back on the line which we had used each year to get us from Brotton to Whitby and Robin Hoods Bay in the 1950's.

In the early part of the new millennium, changes began to take place on the lower promenade, including the provision of new buildings associated with leisure activities close to the cliff tram, and water sports including surfing and jet-skis began to take centre stage in the area around the lower promenade. I might have smiled when someone suggested that Saltburn was aiming to become the 'surfing capital' of the North East – smiled because of my memories of the resort in the 1950's and 1960's – but I was sure at the time that the idea was right and I applauded the aims of the planners and residents who sought to move Saltburn into the twenty-first century. And if confirmation were needed on the vision for the town, I noted recently that Saltburn was named by a national newspaper as one of the UK's top ten surfing hotspots!

# MYSTERY KNITTING AND BRASS BANDS –

## SALTBURN TODAY

I have lost count of the number of times I have visited Saltburn since the turn of the millennium. Forty or fifty times perhaps? As a former 'southern softie', I have not been back to Saltburn in winter since the 1980's, but I have experienced most types of weather on my regular visits during the spring, summer and autumn - sun, rain, thunder, mist, heat, cold, calm, wind – I've seen them all!

It was in August 2015 that I paid my final three visits to the town for the purposes of this book, and on these occasions, I wrote down what I saw. This is what I recorded.

My first visit was on a Monday at the start of the school holidays. The day was sunny and warm – what a change compared with the 1960's – and I was glad to get to the town early, with many cars already parked on Marine Parade, clearly attracted by the sun and absence of car parking charges (long may that continue). Having parked outside my beloved Crake Hall House, for almost twenty years now part of a residential care home, I walked up Ruby Street to find that the Social Club had been demolished and the site was starting to be re-developed. Unsurprising perhaps, but undoubtedly a loss to those who remembered it from its heyday.

Back down on the upper promenade, I looked at the huge wind turbines towards Redcar and the mouth of the River Tees. I counted 27, there might have been more, and these were structures which were definitely not part of the skyline in the 1950's and 1960's.

Having consumed my sandwiches (wholemeal but with cheese slices as in the 1950's!) and taken a look at the old Sea View Guest House on Marine Parade, now a Care Home, I decided to walk via the allotments towards Marske and then back along the sands to Saltburn, the tide being out until late in the afternoon. The Holiday Park, with its lodges for sale at £100,000 +, had taken over some of the rather dowdy caravan park which I remembered from my earlier days at Saltburn, but the extensive allotments remained largely unchanged and it was good to see people of all ages working on them. A two-coach 'Pacer' diesel train hurried past on its way into Saltburn – no steam trains to view today – and soon I was heading down past a housing estate and on to the sands near Marske. At this point, I turned left to take a look at St Germain's Church, or at least what remained of it, the main body of the building having been demolished in the 1950's. It was years since I had last visited the site, and I was greatly impressed with the quiet, well-tended graveyard overlooking the sea, with countless memorial stones remembering those who had died long ago and more recently. The volunteers who maintain the site to this day are to be commended for their work.

It was then back on the sands, with parents and grandparents in shorts and trainers (no suits, ties and coats visible today) shepherding their youngsters on to the beach for an afternoon's fun in the warm sun. The walk back along the 'fine beach' to Saltburn, which my father had enjoyed in the 1920's and 1930's, was undertaken at a stroll and soon the sights and sounds of people enjoying themselves at Saltburn could be heard. If there were fewer people on the beach than I had anticipated, the reasons for this quickly became evident – thick seaweed, and masses of it - all along the beach adjacent to the lower promenade. Seaweed, although unwelcome, has always been a part of life in the resort, and it was good to see that the authorities had cleared away the latest mounds by the time I next visited the beach a couple of weeks later.

After a welcome cup of coffee, in a plastic rather than china cup, I ventured on to the pier, past the well-used amusement arcade of old, to see the 'mystery knitting', an integral part of pier life since 2012. Previously I had seen exhibits to do with the Olympics and World Cup, this time the theme was Alice in Wonderland, whose 150th anniversary was being celebrated in 2015. I am not sure whether the mystery of the 'mystery knitter' has ever been solved, but whoever is responsible is to be congratulated on bringing a new and popular (and free!) venture to the pier and resort.

Moving through the crowds of people on the lower promenade and past the surfing shops and people queuing for fish and chips, I made my way to my beloved Saltburn Miniature Railway in its new location across the beck. Being a Monday, the Railway was not unfortunately in operation, but I was able to see the Railway's new steam engine being tested outside the shed. It was good to see the name Blacklock R already on the side of the engine. Reg Blacklock was a long-time resident of Saltburn, and long-serving and popular member of the Miniature Railway and of the North Yorkshire Moors Railway, and I was pleased that I had been able to chat with him before he died, I wish we had had more time.

The boats and paddling pool by the beck had long disappeared but I was pleased to see lots of children enjoying themselves in the recently completed play area under where the old Halfpenny Bridge crossed the valley. On towards the Italian Gardens I walked alongside the beck in which children were happily playing. The beck was no more than a trickle on that warm summer's afternoon, but I was minded that it can change in no time at all after heavy rain, most notably recently in the widely reported and recorded flash-floods of September 2013, which caused widespread damage in the area.

I sat for a short while in the Italian Gardens, as pristine as I remember them of old, and then it was on along the Valley Gardens walk towards the railway viaduct, a walk which my mum and dad had undertaken in 1941, before turning back along the road to the railway station. My purpose in going to the station was not to catch a train but to get some cash from the cash machine and to purchase some milk - using the automated checkout facility - from the supermarket on the old platform 1. How times have changed! It only remained for me to cross the car park, located on the site of the excursion platform where trains from

Blackpool had disgorged their passengers in times of old, walk down Ruby Street, treading carefully past the unwelcome 'dog-poo', and back to the car at the end of my first August visit to Saltburn. I was exhausted!

My other two visits to Saltburn were made on Sundays. On my first visit, I particularly wanted to see an exhibition in the community centre of Saltburn's involvement in two World Wars, and I was certainly not disappointed with what I saw.

Moving down to the lower promenade, I noticed children riding donkeys on the beach, a timeless activity which of course I remembered from my childhood holidays in the 1950's.

Heading across the beck, I arrived at the miniature railway just as a train, headed by my beloved Prince Charles, was loading for the journey alongside the beck to the Italian Gardens. The cheery driver (I didn't unfortunately manage to get his name) must have wondered why a fairly elderly gentleman on his own was so keen to get photos of the engine and train! It was good to see the train and adjacent car parks so full, and clearly Saltburn was alive and well on a sunny Sunday afternoon!

Music from above could be heard in the valley and I headed back up the hill to pick up the last half-hour or so of the brass band which plays each Sunday afternoon during the summer at the bandstand adjacent to the entrance of the old Halfpenny Bridge. On this occasion, the music was provided by the Lockwood Brass, and the crowds of people sitting in chairs and deckchairs round the bandstand certainly bore testament to the popularity of this weekly activity.

At the conclusion of this particular afternoon, there was a short commemoration at the War Memorial for those from Saltburn who had died in two World Wars and subsequently in action. One of the memorial plaques was for a James Robson of Ruby Street who died at Ypres 100 years ago in May 1915. What, I wonder, was Ruby Street like when James and his comrades marched off to war? I am glad I attended.

On my other Sunday visit, I headed straight out across Huntcliff on foot to the railway line which I had travelled along in the 1950's and again in more recent years. This was a lovely and popular walk on a warm Sunday afternoon. The railway line to the Boulby Mine seemed to be as close to the edge of Huntcliff as I remembered it in the 1950's. Sadly, there were no Sunday trains on the line to admire, so having taken a look at the metal sculptures on the cliff top, I headed back towards Saltburn, enjoying the fine views of the town and along the coast to Redcar and beyond as I returned.

The Royal National Lifeboat Institution were having a collection day in Saltburn and as I came to the steps leading down from Huntcliff, there was sudden activity as the lifeboat was called out from along the coast to rescue a man and his dog from the incoming tide on the rocks under Huntcliff. The accompanying jet-skis may not have been on hand to help in the 1950's or 1960's, but the lifeboat rescue confirmed the timeless and constant need for vigilance in a seaside location such as Saltburn, even on a warm sunny Sunday afternoon. My money went into the RNLI collection box before I headed back to Whitby at the end of my last visit to Saltburn in August 2015 and my last visit for the purposes of this book.

The former station entrance, much as I remember it from
the 1950's, and an arrival at platform 2 does brisk business

The old platform 1 at Saltburn station, with the modern
railway mosaics in the foreground

...and looking towards the former Zetland Hotel

Gosnay's Butchers continue to trade at the top of Ruby Street

...and this is Ruby Street in 2015 from outside Gosnay's

A page for former guest houses in Ruby Street – No 38...

...and No 35

And a page for former guest houses on Marine Parade
- Sea View...

...and Crake Hall House

Brisk business on the promenade on a warm summer's day...

...and the popular 'mystery knitting' on the pier

No passengers at the former Cat Nab station...

...but Prince Charles has a full train as it passes
the new engine shed

The cliff tram also does brisk business

The brass band plays and the town crier cries aloud!

The donkeys wait for business...

...but by then, the crowds have all gone home!

# AND THAT IS SALTBURN 2015

# HARD BEDS AND
# WEEKLY BATHS? –
## SALTBURN AND THE FUTURE

I am sure there must be residents of Saltburn who wondered whether there was any future for the resort when holidaymakers, including my family, began to desert the town, the hotels and guest houses closed down and were converted into flats, and the realities of a new financial climate in the resort and area in general became evident. Certainly I wondered that on my visits to the town in the 1970's and early 1980's.

Perhaps it was a decision to focus on Saltburn's Victorian heritage, with its attendant Victorian Weeks, which started to turn things around in the 1980's, I cannot be sure. However I am certain that Saltburn has benefitted from embracing change, as evidenced by the crowds of people in the resort on each of my three visits there in August 2015. No, I do not imagine that any of them arrived by train for a 2-3 week stay in a local guesthouse with hard beds and weekly baths, but still they came, and the resort caters for their modern needs, with reasonable car parking facilities around the town, toilets that are clean, cafes on the lower promenade where one can sit and watch the world go by, surfing and jet-skis available nearby for the more adventurous, and good shops and café/restaurant facilities around the town including at least one recently reviewed in a national newspaper. Saltburn may have focussed on its Victorian heritage but it has also adapted to the modern day, and those responsible are to be congratulated on their achievements.

Will this continue? Yes, I am sure it will. I missed the Food Festival in 2015, I must try and attend another year. I managed to catch a bit of the annual Folk Weekend in 2014 and noted how popular it was. And I would have liked to have seen the Historic Motor Gathering in September 2015, including a Hill Climb Event on Saltburn Bank, a focus in the modern day on times long ago. These are just three of the events which took place in Saltburn in the summer of 2015, in no small part due, I am sure, to enthusiasm and willingness to get things done in the town.

There is a Community & Arts Association, Studios and Gallery including workshops and events, a monthly Farmers' Market, and the Valley Gardens are looked after (in the main) by volunteer 'friends' who run events including a summer picnic and mini folk & blues festivals.

For rail enthusiasts like myself, the Saltburn Line User Group (SLUG) looks after the interests of passengers on the Saltburn line, and I enjoyed their photographic exhibition in the town in 2011, whilst Saltburn Railtours organise rail trips to different destinations including a long weekend in Bournemouth in 2016.

Roads and transport links to the town are, I suggest, far better than they were in my childhood, and even if I hanker at times after the old days of steam trains to Thornaby and Darlington and round Huntcliff to Whitby, I cannot criticise the regular train and bus services which now bring crowds of people to the resort on a summer Sunday from places such as Middlesbrough, Darlington and beyond.

Sadly, at the time of writing, the area and nation are having to come to terms with the ending of steelmaking at Redcar. I am sure this will impact on the residents of Saltburn and my sympathies go out to those affected. However I am also sure that Saltburn will recover from any downturn in its fortunes, as it has done in the past, and that there is a future for Saltburn, and a very good future at that, which I hope to experience for some years to come.

Oh, and the purpose for writing this book? Well, I recently became a state pensioner and, like my dad before me, I wanted to get my memories down on paper before they fade too much. I am sure you will understand and I hope you will forgive my digressions into adult memories of Saltburn later in the book!

Thank you for reading this book, I hope you have enjoyed it and that it may have brought back some memories for you of the North Yorkshire town called Saltburn-by-the-Sea which I have known and loved over the past 65 years.

Saltburn 1954...

...and the same spot 61 years later!